WEDDING
OF

....

&

....

IF FOUND, PLEASE RETURN TO:

Name:

Address:

Cell Phone: **FAX:**

Work Phone: **FAX:**

Primary E-Mail:

Secondary E-Mail:

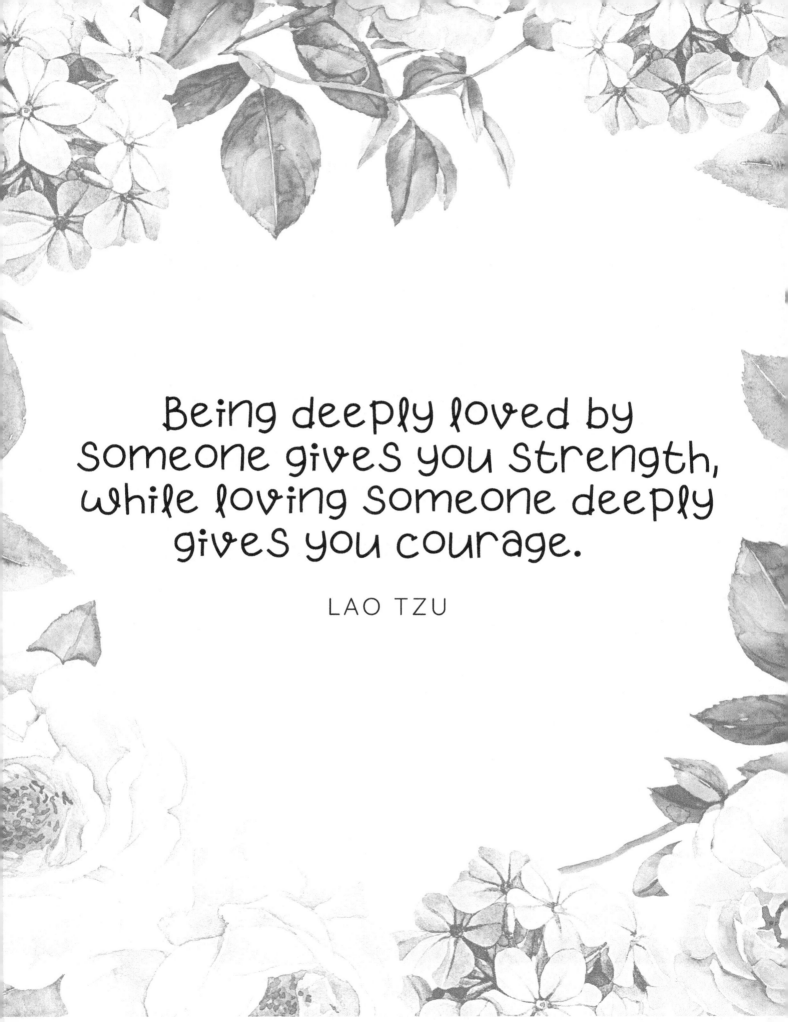

Being deeply loved by
someone gives you strength,
while loving someone deeply
gives you courage.

LAO TZU

Save the Date

Wedding date:

_____

Ceremony venue:

_____

Program Time:

_____

Wedding Contact

WEDDING PLANNER

Name:
Address:

Phone:
Web:

RECEPTION VENUE

Name:
Address:

Phone:
Web:

CEREMONY VENUE

Name:
Address:

Phone:
Web:

OFFICIANT

Name:
Address:

Phone:
Web:

PHOTOGRAPHER

Name:
Address:

Phone:
Web:

VIDEOGRAPHER

Name:
Address:

Phone:
Web:

Wedding Contact

FLORIST

Name:

Address:

Phone:

Web:

BAKER

Name:

Address:

Phone:

Web:

CATERER

Name:

Address:

Phone:

Web:

TRANSPORTATION

Name:

Address:

Phone:

Web:

DJ/ ENTERTAINMENT

Name:

Address:

Phone:

Web:

LIGHTING COMPANY

Name:

Address:

Phone:

Web:

Wedding Contact

BRIDAL DRESS

Name:

Address:

Phone:

Web:

MAKEUP ARTIST

Name:

Address:

Phone:

Web:

HAIR STYLIST

Name:

Address:

Phone:

Web:

JEWELER

Name:

Address:

Phone:

Web:

STATIONARY DESIGNER

Name:

Address:

Phone:

Web:

HONEYMOON RESORT

Name:

Address:

Phone:

Web:

Order of Events

PRIORITY	DATE & TIME	EVENT	SONG

Order of Events

PRIORITY	DATE & TIME	EVENT	SONG

Dates to Remember

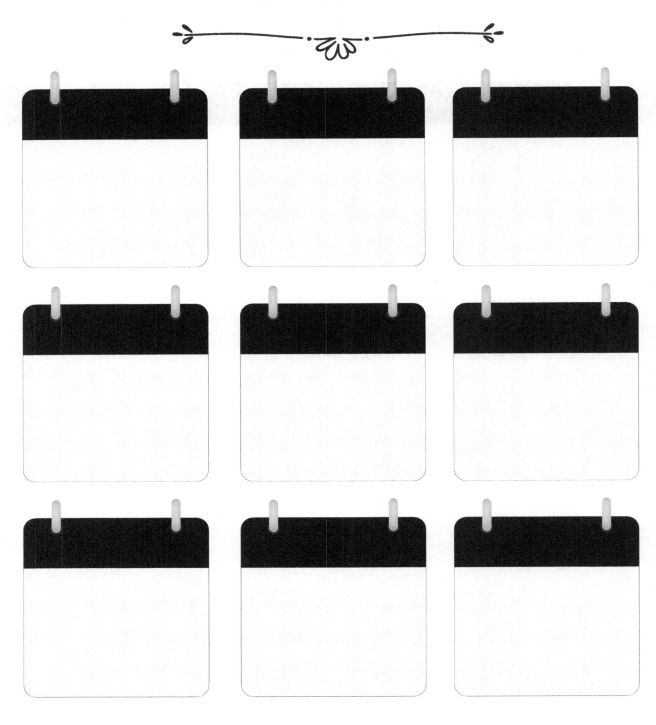

Notes: _____

_____

_____

_____

Dates to Remember

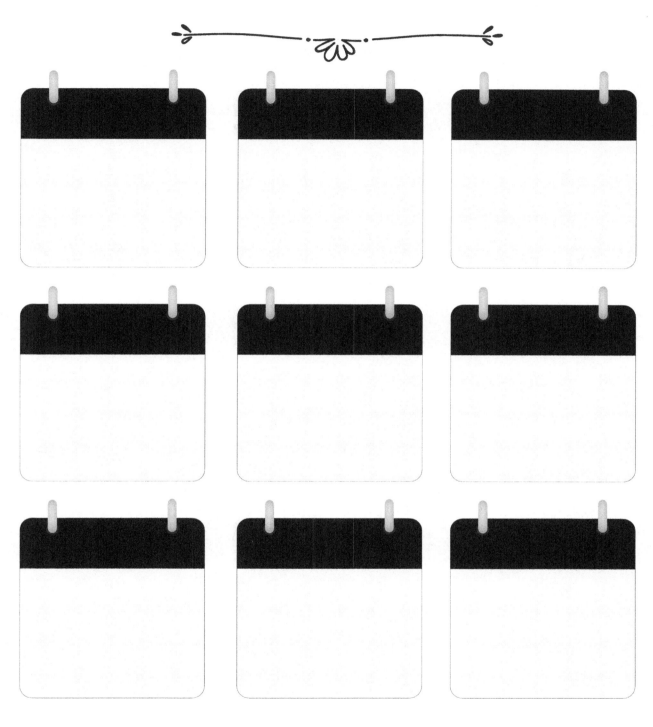

Notes:
_____

_____

_____

_____

Dates to Remember

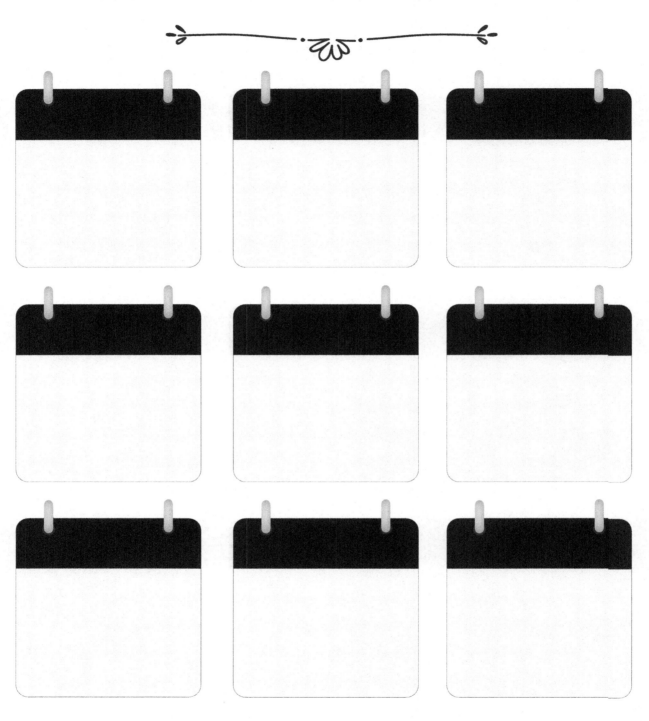

Notes: _____

_____

_____

_____

Dates to Remember

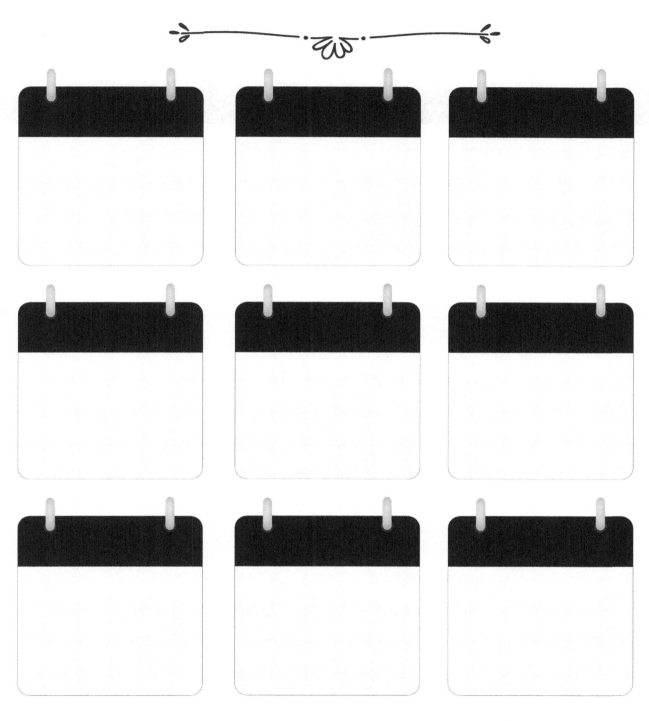

Notes:
_____
_____
_____
_____

Address Book

ROLE	NAME AND CONTACT INFORMATION
Maid of Honor	
Best Man	

Address Book

ROLE	NAME AND CONTACT INFORMATION

Song List

EVENT	SONG TITLE	ARTIST	VERSION

Song List

EVENT	SONG TITLE	ARTIST	VERSION

Guest List

NAME	CONTACT INFORMATION	RSVP
		☐
		☐
		☐
		☐
		☐
		☐
		☐
		☐
		☐
		☐
		☐

Guest List

NAME	CONTACT INFORMATION	RSVP
		☐
		☐
		☐
		☐
		☐
		☐
		☐
		☐
		☐
		☐
		☐

Guest List

NAME	CONTACT INFORMATION	RSVP
		☐
		☐
		☐
		☐
		☐
		☐
		☐
		☐
		☐
		☐
		☐

Guest List

NAME	CONTACT INFORMATION	RSVP
		☐
		☐
		☐
		☐
		☐
		☐
		☐
		☐
		☐
		☐
		☐

Guest List

NAME	CONTACT INFORMATION	RSVP
		☐
		☐
		☐
		☐
		☐
		☐
		☐
		☐
		☐
		☐
		☐

Guest List

NAME	CONTACT INFORMATION	RSVP
		☐
		☐
		☐
		☐
		☐
		☐
		☐
		☐
		☐
		☐
		☐

Guest List

NAME	CONTACT INFORMATION	RSVP
		☐
		☐
		☐
		☐
		☐
		☐
		☐
		☐
		☐
		☐
		☐

Guest List

NAME	CONTACT INFORMATION	RSVP
		☐
		☐
		☐
		☐
		☐
		☐
		☐
		☐
		☐
		☐
		☐

Seating Chart

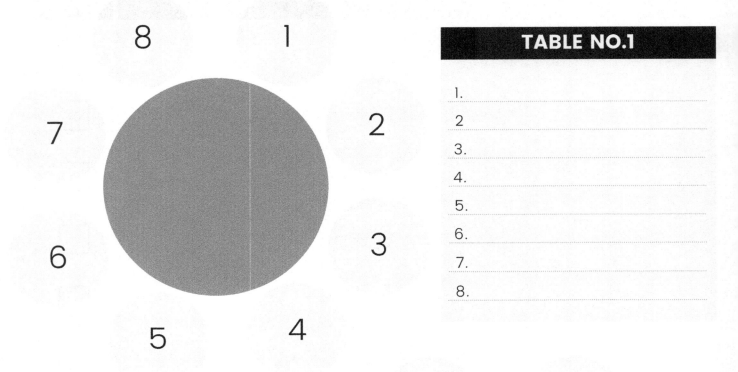

8   1

7

6

2

3

5   4

TABLE NO.1

1.
2.
3.
4.
5.
6.
7.
8.

TABLE NO.2

1.
2.
3.
4.
5.
6.
7.
8.

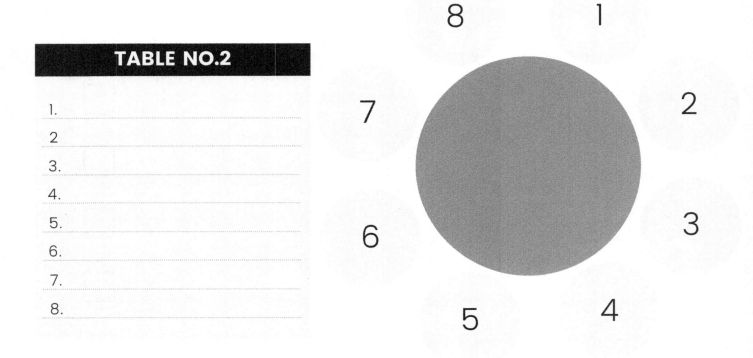

8   1

7

6

2

3

5   4

Seating Chart

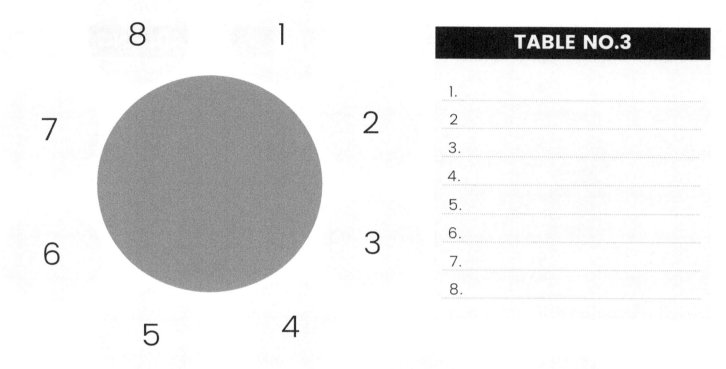

8   1

7

6

5   4

2

3

TABLE NO.3

1.
2
3.
4.
5.
6.
7.
8.

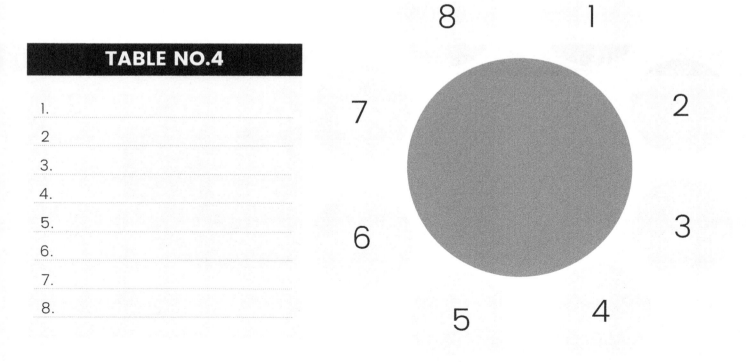

TABLE NO.4

1.
2
3.
4.
5.
6.
7.
8.

8   1

7

6

5   4

2

3

Seating Chart

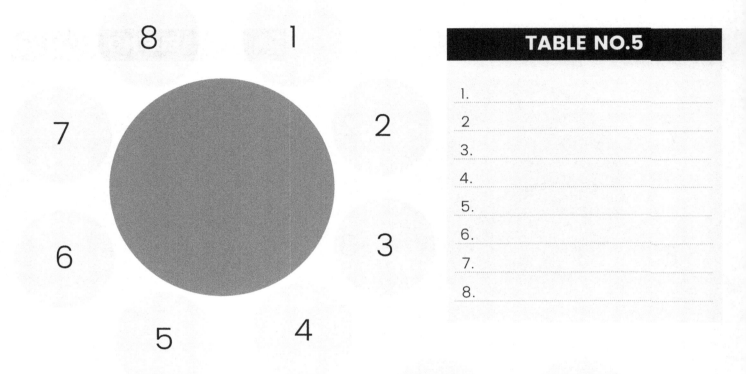

8　　　　　　1

7

6

2

3

5　　　　4

TABLE NO.5

1. ....
2 ....
3. ....
4. ....
5. ....
6. ....
7. ....
8. ....

TABLE NO.6

1. ....
2 ....
3. ....
4. ....
5. ....
6. ....
7. ....
8. ....

8　　　　　　1

7

6

2

3

5　　　　4

Seating Chart

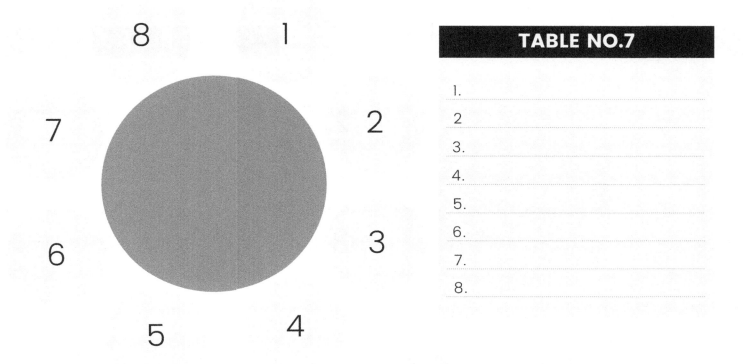

8   1

7

6

5   4

2

3

TABLE NO.7

1.
2
3.
4.
5.
6.
7.
8.

TABLE NO.8

1.
2
3.
4.
5.
6.
7.
8.

8   1

7

6

5   4

2

3

Seating Chart

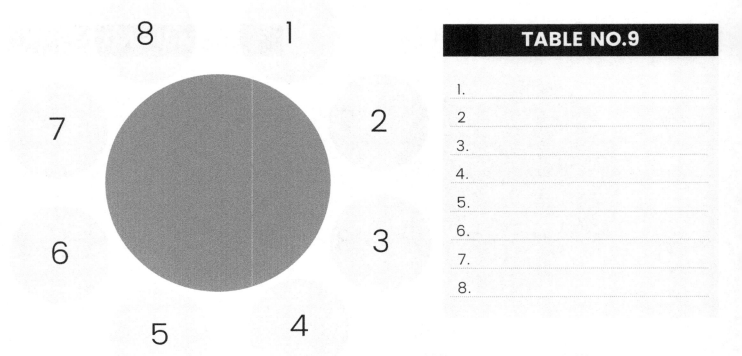

8   1

7

6

5   4

8   1

7   2

6   3

5   4

Seating Chart

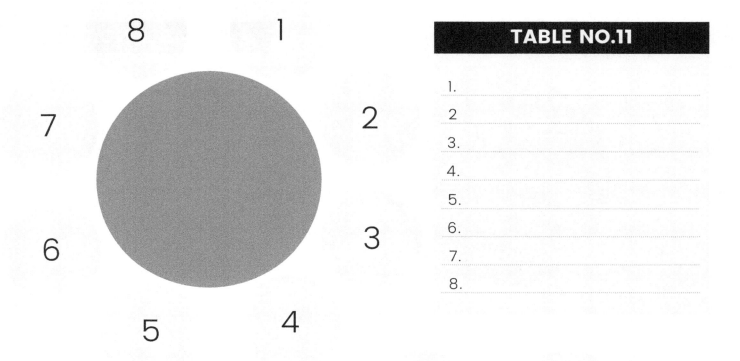

8   1

7

2

6

3

5   4

TABLE NO.11

1. ....
2 ....
3. ....
4. ....
5. ....
6. ....
7. ....
8. ....

TABLE NO.12

1. ....
2 ....
3. ....
4. ....
5. ....
6. ....
7. ....
8. ....

8   1

7

2

6

3

5   4

Seating Chart

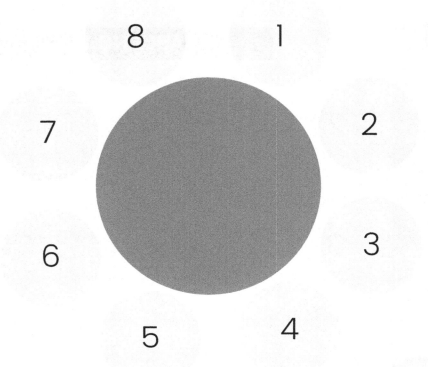

8 1

7

6

5 4

2

3

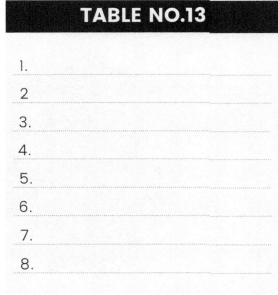

TABLE NO.13

1. _____
2. _____
3. _____
4. _____
5. _____
6. _____
7. _____
8. _____

TABLE NO.14

1. _____
2. _____
3. _____
4. _____
5. _____
6. _____
7. _____
8. _____

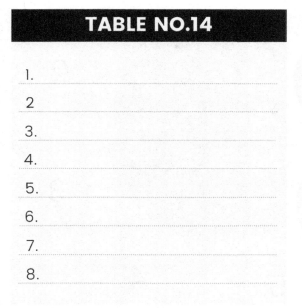

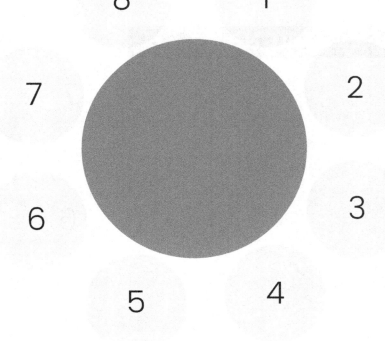

8 1

7

6

5 4

2

3

Seating Chart

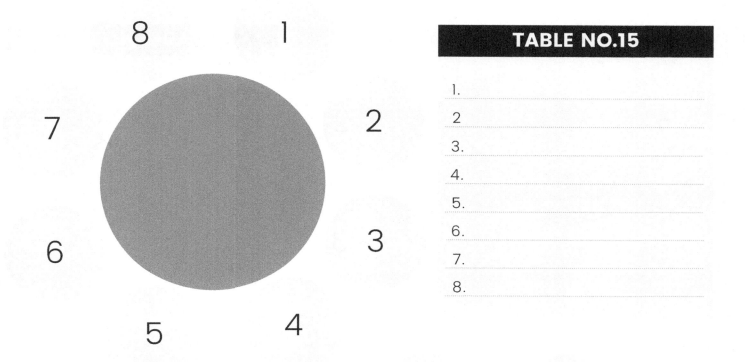

8   1

7

6

5   4

2

3

TABLE NO.15

1. _____
2. _____
3. _____
4. _____
5. _____
6. _____
7. _____
8. _____

8   1

7

6

5   4

2

3

TABLE NO.16

1. _____
2. _____
3. _____
4. _____
5. _____
6. _____
7. _____
8. _____

Seating Chart

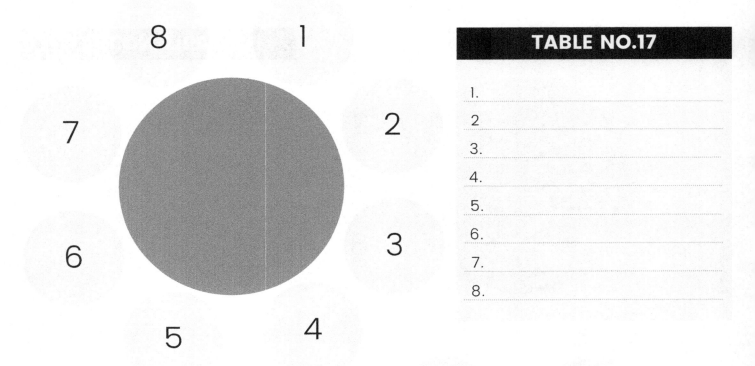

TABLE NO.17

1. _____
2. _____
3. _____
4. _____
5. _____
6. _____
7. _____
8. _____

TABLE NO.18

1. _____
2. _____
3. _____
4. _____
5. _____
6. _____
7. _____
8. _____

Wedding Budget

DETAILS	ESTIMATE	COST	DEPOSIT	LEFT

Wedding Budget

DETAILS	ESTIMATE	COST	DEPOSIT	LEFT

Wedding Budget

DETAILS	ESTIMATE	COST	DEPOSIT	LEFT

Wedding Budget

DETAILS	ESTIMATE	COST	DEPOSIT	LEFT

Wedding Budget

DETAILS	ESTIMATE	COST	DEPOSIT	LEFT

Wedding Budget

DETAILS	ESTIMATE	COST	DEPOSIT	LEFT

Wedding Budget

DETAILS	ESTIMATE	COST	DEPOSIT	LEFT

Wedding Budget

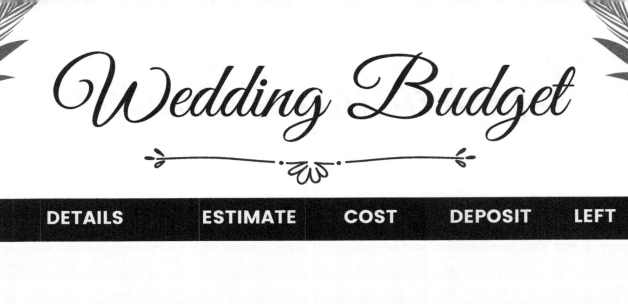

DETAILS	ESTIMATE	COST	DEPOSIT	LEFT

Wedding Budget

DETAILS	ESTIMATE	COST	DEPOSIT	LEFT

Wedding Budget

DETAILS	ESTIMATE	COST	DEPOSIT	LEFT

Notes

Notes

Notes

Notes

Notes

Notes

Notes

Notes

Notes

Notes

Notes

Notes

Notes

Notes

Notes

Notes

Notes

Notes

Notes

Notes

Notes

Notes

Notes

Notes

Notes

Notes

To Do List

To Do List

To Do List

To Do List

To Do List

- ♡ ....
- ♡ ....
- ♡ ....
- ♡ ....
- ♡ ....
- ♡ ....
- ♡ ....
- ♡ ....
- ♡ ....
- ♡ ....

To Do List

To Do List

To Do List

To Do List

To Do List

- ♥ ....
- ♥ ....
- ♥ ....
- ♥ ....
- ♥ ....
- ♥ ....
- ♥ ....
- ♥ ....
- ♥ ....
- ♥ ....
- ♥ ....

To Do List

To Do List

- ♡ ....
- ♡ ....
- ♡ ....
- ♡ ....
- ♡ ....
- ♡ ....
- ♡ ....
- ♡ ....
- ♡ ....
- ♡ ....

To Do List

To Do List

To Do List

To Do List

- ♡ ....
- ♡ ....
- ♡ ....
- ♡ ....
- ♡ ....
- ♡ ....
- ♡ ....
- ♡ ....
- ♡ ....
- ♡ ....
- ♡ ....

To Do List

To Do List

To Do List

To Do List

- ♡ ....
- ♡ ....
- ♡ ....
- ♡ ....
- ♡ ....
- ♡ ....
- ♡ ....
- ♡ ....
- ♡ ....
- ♡ ....
- ♡ ....

To Do List

To Do List

To Do List

To Do List

To Do List

- ❤ ....
- ❤ ....
- ❤ ....
- ❤ ....
- ❤ ....
- ❤ ....
- ❤ ....
- ❤ ....
- ❤ ....
- ❤ ....
- ❤ ....

To Do List

- ♡ ....
- ♡ ....
- ♡ ....
- ♡ ....
- ♡ ....
- ♡ ....
- ♡ ....
- ♡ ....
- ♡ ....
- ♡ ....
- ♡ ....

To Do List

To Do List

- ♡ ....
- ♡ ....
- ♡ ....
- ♡ ....
- ♡ ....
- ♡ ....
- ♡ ....
- ♡ ....
- ♡ ....
- ♡ ....
- ♡ ....

To Do List

WHERE THERE IS
LOVE
there is life